Where I Live
My Street

by Meg Gaertner

www.focusreaders.com

Copyright © 2021 by Focus Readers®, Lake Elmo, MN 55042. All rights reserved. No part of this book may be reproduced or utilized in any form or by any means without written permission from the publisher.

Focus Readers is distributed by North Star Editions:
sales@northstareditions.com | 888-417-0195

Produced for Focus Readers by Red Line Editorial.

Photographs ©: Shutterstock Images, cover, 1, 15; iStockphoto, 4, 7, 9, 11 (top), 11 (bottom), 13 (top), 13 (bottom), 16 (top left), 16 (top right), 16 (bottom left), 16 (bottom right)

Library of Congress Cataloging-in-Publication Data
Names: Gaertner, Meg, author.
Title: My street / Meg Gaertner.
Description: Lake Elmo, MN : Focus Readers, 2021. | Series: Where I live | Includes index. | Audience: Grades K–1
Identifiers: LCCN 2019054801 (print) | LCCN 2019054802 (ebook) | ISBN 9781644933411 (hardcover) | ISBN 9781644934173 (paperback) | ISBN 9781644935699 (pdf) | ISBN 9781644934937 (ebook)
Subjects: LCSH: Neighborhoods--Juvenile literature. | Streets--Juvenile literature. | Vocabulary--Juvenile literature.
Classification: LCC HM761 .G34 2021 (print) | LCC HM761 (ebook) | DDC 307.3/362--dc23
LC record available at https://lccn.loc.gov/2019054801
LC ebook record available at https://lccn.loc.gov/2019054802

Printed in the United States of America
Mankato, MN
082020

About the Author

Meg Gaertner is a children's book editor and author. She lives in Minneapolis, Minnesota. When not writing, she is usually dancing or spending time outside.

Table of Contents

On My Street 5

My Neighbors 8

At the Park 12

Glossary 16

Index 16

house

yard

On My Street

I live on a street.

There are many houses.

The houses have yards.

There are also apartments.

Many families live in one building.

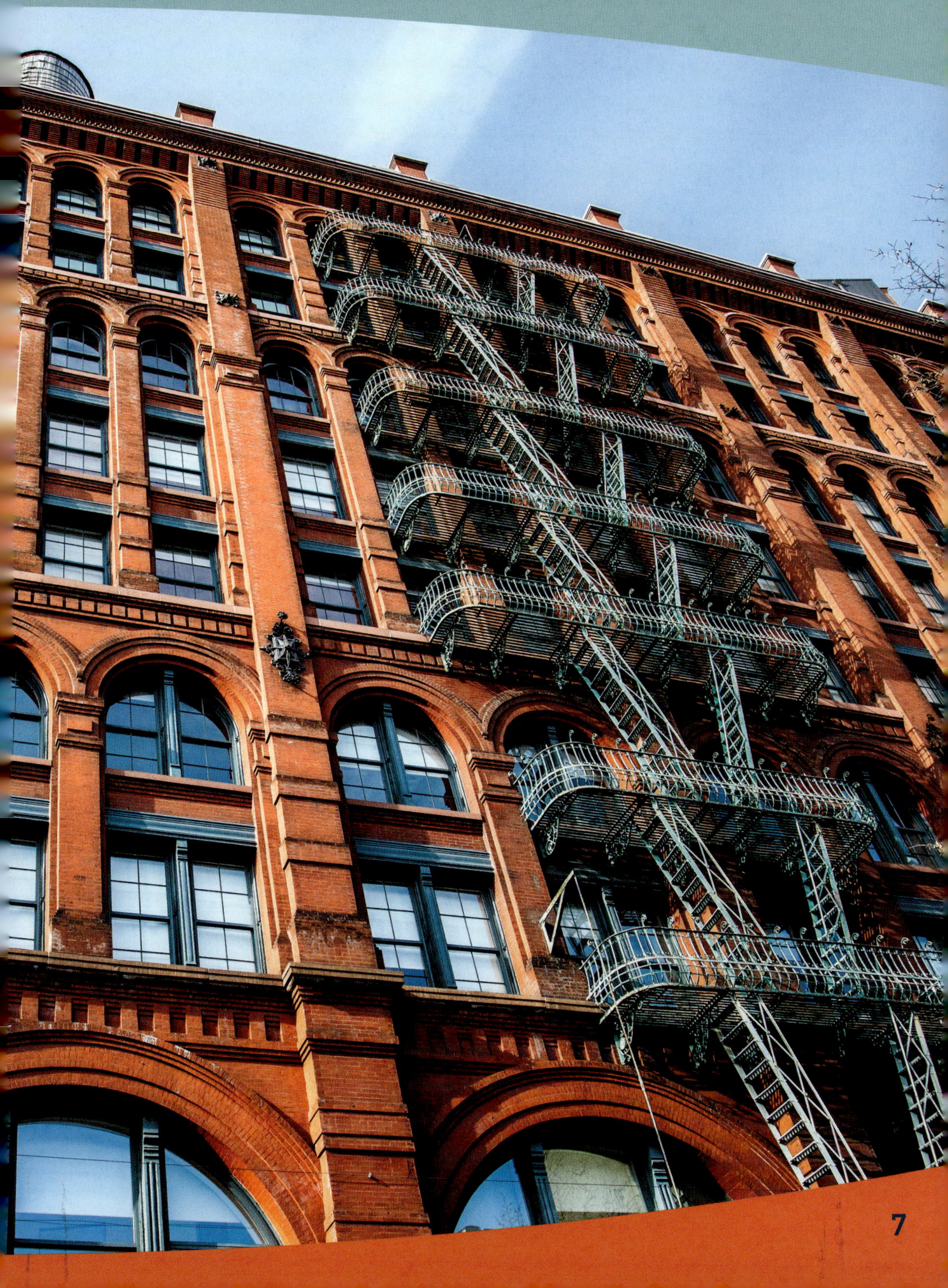

My Neighbors

Many people live on my street.

They are my neighbors.

They walk on the **sidewalk**.

They walk their dogs.

sidewalk

People drive in cars.

They drive down the street.

They stop at the **stop sign**.

car

stop sign

11

At the Park

My street has a park.

People have fun at the park.

They go on the **swings**.

They go down the **slide**.

swings

slide

I play games at the park.

I play with my neighbors.

Glossary

sidewalk

stop sign

slide

swings

Index

A
apartments, 6

H
houses, 5

N
neighbors, 8, 14

P
park, 12, 14